Heart Paraphernalia

God won't let your Heart accept the paraphernalia of Love

IamKnowOne

authorHOUSE

AuthorHouse™
1663 Liberty Drive
Bloomington, IN 47403
www.authorhouse.com
Phone: 1 (800) 839-8640

Published by AuthorHouse 05/13/2020

ISBN: 978-1-7283-6159-8 (sc)
ISBN: 978-1-7283-6158-1 (e)

Library of Congress Control Number: 2020908549

Print information available on the last page.

Any people depicted in stock imagery provided by Getty Images are models, and such images are being used for illustrative purposes only.
Certain stock imagery © Getty Images.

This book is printed on acid-free paper.

I'm Going to Make you Fall in Love with the way these Poetic Expressions
are written and released from my Tongue

I'm sorry that I sound Unperturbed and you don't even know my name

Hello IamKnowOne

From the Complexity Of my Vital voice

To the discernment in yours

I'm going to Passionately put words together that will help you Laugh, Think,
Love, Cry, Mend, Motivate, uplift, and Forgive

Smile You Deserve the Best, and Only the Best of Me is what I'll Give.

IamKnowOne..

I'm going to Hit this World with my Poetic Expressions like a Monsoon

The next Poem that I inscribe will always be coming Soon

Or until Death do us Part

I Promise you, I was in Love at first WRITE, now we share a Heart

I will continuously learn and study, keeping my pen on deck on any given Day

I aspire to stay ready, just like the astonishing and gifted Paul Laurence Dunbar when he wrote-A Golden Day

I am a Baltimorean, who aspires to to be as amazing as all of the Greats and fulfill my Dreams

Yet be as inspirational as the astounding and very talented Edgar Allen Poe when he wrote-A Dream Within a Dream

I aspire for my Poems to be as compelling and picturesque as the Phenomenal Maya Angelou as long as I'm Alive

I'll always try my Best to motivate and encourage people as she did when she wrote-And Still I Rise

IamKnowOne..

Good girl gone Bad for Love

But we'll always ride together like two people stuck together in a single latex Glove

She was Driving with one hand backwards doing Eighty on the Highway

But I can close my eyes, I Trust my Bae

With endless Love, shared Hearts and shared Fingerprints will dissolve Evidence

So Our love will always be Relevant

And I will consistently love her wholeheartedly remaining humble with no Arrogance

My Good Girl My Bad Girl

We'll forever be as One in this World

IamKnowOne....

Who am I to question God

When he puts me at a certain place at a certain Time

Who am I to question God

When he's showing me where my heart needs to be at that point in Time

Who am I to question God

When I can't sleep because I'm Stressed throughout the Night

Who am I to question God

Although cancer Won and my Mom lost the Fight

Who am I to question God

When he gives me eyes to see when someone is doing me wrong, and I act like I lost my Sight

Who am I to question God

When he gave me the Power to Love, and they chose not to act Right

Who am I to question God

When I had the Gun to my head, and the word Dad saved my Life

Never will I question God

Who am I, His Humbled Servant for Life

Thank You God

IamKnowOne..

I was so Amazed by your Grace

That it was hard for me to come to Grips

Than I really felt like I could taste that cherry red lipstick placed so gracefully upon your Lips

As I watched you Work the room with one hand placed so gracefully upon your Hips

I knew in a few minutes that you would have to take your Seat

But I'm Loving the way that you're walking in them Heels, placed so gracefully upon your Feet

Tonight Tonight Tonight, I feel so euphoric simply being in the same Place that you're In

Because Your Grace is So Amazing

IamKnowOne..

There is an Unequivocal Connection between Us

I can't say it's Love, but it's Far from Lust

You seem just as interested as I am, you're very Confident yet Extremely Shy

But you're very Beautiful so it's probably Hard for you to Express yourself to any Guy

Or maybe you've been Hurt Before

So you Try your Best to Hold on to your Feelings until your absolutely Sure

I get It sometimes we all are afraid of the Unknown

But if we let the Right one go, do we just settle give up on Happiness, Lie to ourselves, keep a smile on the outside

Knowing that Inside we really feel Alone

If you Know that person makes you Happy Live your Best Life and stay the Fuck out of the Comfort Zone

IamKnowOne..

I've been Crushing on you since day One

And from that look in your eyes, I Could've swore you said Damn, I would love to have your Son

But seriously, I was Never Star struck by Beautiful women in magazines or on TV

But the first time I saw you, I had to Run to the bathroom and it wasn't because I had to Pee

I always thought I was a cool Dude, and never had a lack for words in all of my Days

In Real Life, you have to be the reason they came up with Women Crush Wednesdays

Your Beauty makes me Nervous and your Grace keeps me in my Place

Simply thinking of you, keeps my Feelings Alive

Because I'm feeling this Woman Crush Three Sixty Five

IamKnowOne..

How Beautiful could it Be

You and I taking walks, holding hands for everyone to See

How Beautiful could it Be

You and I sitting side by side in church, as the Pastor speaks about being

Happy

How Beautiful could it Be

You keep talking about weight gain, but Love is all I See

How Beautiful could it Be

If the first time we make love, your eyes get filled with Tears

Because you know that I want to hold you so tight, that it'll love away all

of your Fears

Can you look at Me? Damn you're Gorgeous

How's Beautiful could it Be

IamKnowOne..

Love is a Happiness that you've never felt in your Life

Love is knowing she's the One and Making her your Wife

Love is an Everlasting feeling that never leaves your Soul

Love is arguing over Unnecessary things that make you Lose Control

Love is Understanding and taking care of the Needs of your Mate

Love is not Control but a Conversation to Compromise that will keep you up Late

Love is knowing that you did something wrong and doing everything you can to make it Right

Love is falling asleep at night with a pain so deep you lose your Appetite

Love is never making a woman feel Meaningless and always appreciating her Worth

Love is always Making your woman feel like she's the only woman on Earth

Love is showing public Affection just to see her Smile

A gentle Kiss on the Lips or a walk holding hands for a While

Love can Fill your Heart or make it Empty

When do we learn that God may only send us One True Love in a Century

IamKnowOne..

Flowers

I want to be able to Love Her

Hold her as tight as I can, without breaking Her

Because she's as delicate as a petal on a Red Rose

When she's happy, I can tell that her insides are blooming like a gorgeous Amaryllis, it Shows

I don't ever want to hurt her, I want to listen and learn all of the Loving signs that I'm suppose To

Considering I never want to see her face turn Violet Blue

So when I get the chance she'll see that our Love will bloom like Perennials, and each year we can watch the Bleeding Hearts, without having Bleeding Hearts

IamKnowOne..

My Heart palpitates every time I see You

I try to get a word out but I can't control my Breathing, my apologies that's New

You're the type of woman that only comes around once in a Lifetime

And I know you are like a Rare delicate multicolored Rose, and I will do my best to make sure that you don't lose one single Petal

Even during the winter time, because if I hurt you and anyway I might as well cut my Own major blood Vessel

Your existence alone is intimidating but oh so Special

I want you but I'm Afraid

I'm just a man that's so Amazed

The power of a woman, to God I Praise

IamKnowOne..

There was no justification for her annihilation, and it was done without any Ramification

How do you try to destroy a woman's Whole Soul

than have your side, but leave the real story Untold

Love is an obligation, and it should never be mistaken for one's Temptation

Now she's left said, hurt and alone, you lied tried to destroy her Reputation

Left her with all kinds of complications, and now she needs Jesus for Rehabilitation

And out of desperation, Now you want Reconciliation

I'm sure Jesus gave her an answer without Hesitation

Your love for her should have been effortless, for everyone's Observations

But now you need Litigation to give you Representation for your Explanations

Nah.. Homie you got her all Fucked up, and now you want to force her into a Situation

Now my dedication to loving her, will undoubtably be her Elevation

I'll give her motivation and stimulation because God didn't make no mistakes upon her Creation

And If I ever see you, If I Ever, you better run to the nearest cave, and go into Hibernation

Now Karma will be your Realization

Smacking your lying ass in your Whole inner being with the force of a train, without any Discrimination

Facts, My Revelation.

IamKnowOne..

I Strive to be the Best at Whatever it is that I Do

And I be Damn if I Block my Blessings trying to Judge you

I Work to Hard being Assiduous at what I Do

Besides when I Look in the Mirror I see Me not You

So I want to be Absolutely Clear when I look in my Rearview

IamKnowOne..

My Bae makes me want to be the Best man that I can Be

My Bae makes me want this moment to last forever, because I know this is the Last Love for Me

My Bae makes me see the sun shining through a horrific Storm

My Bae got me wanting to close my eyes when I'm around other women, because my heart only sees her, so that's my Norm

So if you see me with my eyes closed, my apologies I'm in my right Mind

My Bae's Love Just got me All the way Blind

Loving Bae.

IamKnowOne..

No woman is perfect, and that's not a Misconception

So After the alluring Connection

He shows you, that you're his Perfection without Exception

Never Rejection

His soul Obsession

From the first Impression

Without you, his life wouldn't have any Direction

When he misses your Affection

He has to control his Erections

He might not have all the answers but when it comes to your Love it's no Questions

Just the notion of you loving him, will always change his Expression

Happiness will be the only Detection

IamKnowOne..

After your Work day is over let me get your slippers and your iPad

Let me listen to the things from today that made you Mad

Let me Massage your feet before I Listen to your Stories

By the way did you hear that Jay Z song Glory

That's a Beautiful thing between a Man and his Wife

To put little Blue Ivy on a song as She begins her Life

Oh for real, your Boss said That

Than I know you said, I can't with you, as you visualized her ass being Smacked

How does that feel is your feet Relaxed

Is that Chipotle I Smell? Let me get you a Tic Tac

Yeah I know I'm a funny Dude but I Love to see you Smile

Let me take care of the Kids while You chill for Awhile

Dinner is Cooking and the Bubble bath is Floating

I put something in the Tub to Massage you while your Soaking

I try my Best to Spoil you and I'm willing to do whatever to Please

So please open up those gorgeous thighs, as I get down on My Knees

IamKnowOne..

If you're in a Relationship and you feel lonely Run

That person just robbed you of your Love without using a Gun

To know you is to Love You

And without you saying a single word,

I should know if you need me to Hold You

And every time that you're not in my presence, just know you'll be Missed

But for now I know that you need this Forehead Kiss

IamKnowOne..

She didn't understand that men from her past had given her PTSD

She said that she wouldn't feel my Whole Love, if she wasn't going to be abused by Me.

She had been through so much pain trying to find Real Love

So when her heart finally felt it, she couldn't Understand

She said if I don't hit her than I'm not a Real Man

So when I didn't oblige, she Ran

She ran and kept running, until she ran into Herself

Than she realized and was absolutely sure that I loved her like no one Else

She asked could we get back together and continue what she had Left

But by the time she came to her reality, I realized that my heart had started running with someone Else

IamKnowOne...

How can I ever expect to have her whole heart, if I don't help take away all
of the pain that the man or men before me has caused
I have to help her Heal
Than all of her Heart will most certainly be a part of the Deal
IamKnowOne...

Her Smile is Contagious

Her Beauty is Ageless

Her Brainpower is Simply Greatness

She Enters A Room so Gracious

Her Body is Outrageous

In a crowd of Intellectuals she's very Loquacious

She's so Sexy and Poised, so She's never Flirtatious

And She makes her Own Money so she's not worried about your Wages..

IamKnowOne..

If you want me I'm yours, Mentally I'm beyond Ready

Emotionally I've never felt my Heart beat so Steady

I want your Feelings floating on clouds Everyday

I'm very competitive, so I have to make sure you've never known Love in such a Way

There isn't a day that goes by, that I don't think of a creative way to blow your Mind

So when we get to that point, I want you to think outside of the Box, while I'm in the Box assuring you that it was meant to be Mines

IamKnowOne..

I Want to be your Lover, your Fighter, your Soulmate, Protecter and Best Friend

I know you're Afraid because you've been Hurt before

But no worries take your time and Earn my Trust before we Begin

We both have Battle wounds from untamed Love

Let's Love each other's pain Away and finally give our Hearts something to be proud Of

IamKnowOne..

Some people talk about you being Over Weight

I personally know that you're Over Great

You've been dealing with people talking about you for Years

Nevertheless you stayed positive, and kept stepping in your Heels with No
Fear

Letting their despicable faces know, that to you, their negativity could Never
Interfere

IamKnowOne..

They say Speak it into Existence

I can tell that you're feeling me, so your Heart will never be my Resistance

And I'm sure you know that my Feelings is ready for Coexistence

It's been a while, and I still show you considerable Persistence

I know you're extremely Curious

Maybe you don't think that I will take you Serious

But Indeed I will, I know that I like to joke talking about my exotic Creativity

that's stuck in my Mind.

My apologies, I have no control over all of your sex appeal but I promise, if

I ever get the chance I'll Love you long Time

Furthermore I can absolutely make sure that I'm provocative only for You

Because I'm to old for Games, and I'd rather Play Russian roulette before

any thought of hurting You

IamKnowOne..

Sometimes we give our Hearts to the wrong One

We allow them to do us wrong, but we keep chasing, like Shadows that follow us under the Sun

Do me a favor Stop, than look around and tell me what you See

A shadow that appears to be very exhausted and a colossal Tree

Ok, if you relax long enough under Gods tree,

the shadow will become harder for you to See

So enjoy the cool breeze and understand that God knows exactly where he wants you to Be

What God has for you, is meant Solely for You

And Yes, Love and Happiness is included in there Too

IamKnowOne..

Thank you for helping me to understand the air that I'm breathing Again

Thank you for helping me truly Hear the words in a love song, and knowing that craving for your love is not a Sin

Thank you for helping me understand that God assuredly wanted me to find love and a new Beginning

That now has no Ending

I appreciate you, Thank you, I love you, I'm so Thankful, and I know that God sincerely wants us to Win

IamKnowOne...

Sometimes you can't Help the way that you Feel

When I think about her, I Smile for no reason, is Cupid truly Real?

I know I felt an instant connection the first day we looked into each other's Eyes

That day has long passed, but every thought of her still lights up my day, and I'm not Surprised

IamKnowOne..

I'm sorry I don't think she's imperious, what I see is Confidence in her Eyes

You have to approach her like a grown man should, but you're probably already thinking about your Lies

I see Maturity, a woman that's far from Stuck Up

You just know if you say the wrong thing to Her, you Than Fucked all the way Up

IamKnowOne..

In Real Life, you're the Only woman that I'm continuously Chasing in my Dreams

I think it's a sign of where my Whole Feelings should be, No In Betweens

IamKnowOne..

Her body makes me feel so demented that I just want to Gently reconstruct her inner Walls

Just the thought of her coming near me, is making me want to Grab her, Choke her, and drive up her Walls

And who told her to keep wearing that Damn Chanel No Five

It makes me want to take her in the parking garage and eat her Ass Alive

If I ever get the chance, I'll patiently put it In

than creatively drive around her Walls as if I have road Rage

Than make her feel so good that she'd wish she read the Whole book on me, not just one damn Page

Start telling her how her aura makes me feel so incredibly Untamed

Start talking very provocatively, as the feeling vividly makes me scream her Name

Start pulling her hair while Whispering in her ear, that now is Not the time to make Love

As we start walking towards the wall and I give her a benevolent Shove

Than I Grab her, pull her closer, and get so excited that I Leave skid marks on her Walls

While her back is up against the walls

Than tell her how her sex appeal is calling the Beast out of Me

As I give her eye contact, while she taps out smiles and makes a considerable Plea

IamKnowOne..

Hey Heavenly, look me in my eyes and tell me what you See

A reflection of yourself, because your soul lives within Me

There's no better place for you on God's earth, than in my Arms

And I Promise, that I'll Die protecting you, before you endure any type of

Harm

Hey you, You are most certainly Heavenly

And I would be out of my Fucking Mind, to act like there's another place

I'd rather Be

IamKnowOne..

Your Body language is Infectious, accompanied by a very Ravishing smile

I Feel like my Life has a New beginning, I never use to smile, but Thinking of you made it a part of my Style

Just the Notion of your Charisma instantly captivates my Heart

I know your Love is what I need until Tell Death do us Part

IamKnowOne...

Em Em Em Brains and Beauty, God has Blessed Me

I will Love you til the death of Me

Until that very moment my soul has left Me

But while I'm here, I'll give you nothing less than the Best of Me

Wait a minute, did you see that? I think an Angel just flew by and said that

we were destined to Be

Until death do us Part

I'm going to Love you so hard, that you'll think it's Impossible, for death to

do us Part

Because as soon as my soul leaves my body, it's going straight to your Heart

IamKnowOne..

Hey Lady why are you on the Floor Crying

OH He Hurt You Again

But Crying on the Floor is Only Letting that Bastard Win

Look at you, You're Gorgeous and your Tears are Messing up your Dress

I DON'T CARE, I just Wish My Brother was here so He could Lay his Ass Down to Rest

I did Everything for that Bastard, I cooked, cleaned Sucked and Pleased However He wanted to be Pleased

That Trifling Ass Hole Only wanted to Deceived

Now My Heart is Hurting and I'm starting to feel like I can't Breathe

I Hate his Lying Ass, All He did was Deceive

I Know you Don't want to Hear this right Now

But Some things are just Meant to Be

Sometimes We have to Endure Pain just so we can See

I Promise You Time Heals all Wounds

So Get up please when you do Good you get Good

Someone Will come along and Treat your Sexy Ass Amazing Real Soon.

Real Love Exist, We just have to STOP trying to make it Work with the Wrong Person

Let's go, no more Hurting

IamKnowOne..

Hold on it's Coming

Amazing days and Joyous Nights

Hold on is Coming

Financial freedom and the Love of your Life

Hold on it's Coming

You've endured all of the devils Pain

Now God is about to walk you straight up out of the Flames

Hold on it's Coming

Sometimes you think you're praying for no Reason

But Hold on God can change your life over night, like the start of a new Season

Hold on it's Coming

Sometimes I know you feel like life is giving you more than you can handle, and you'd rather jump into a lions Den

Hold on it's Coming

God will never let you down, so bow down and thank him for your Life and keep talking to him until you're ready to say Amen

HOLD ON ITS COMING

Amen

IamKnowOne...

The way she Rocks her beautiful bald head is very Appealing

When your confidence is high, you'll have no Ceilings

Feeling unbothered by the strange Looks

Because she's Stepping so Debonair in those Heels, that it's making everyone

Look

As she smiles, out of nowhere Photons shines over her entire Body

Than her melanin had this amazing radiance, as if angels wanted everyone

to See

At that moment, I know she wanted to scream out, Fuck others opinions, it's

just Sublime being Me

IamKnowOne..

The sound of your Voice is very Unsurpassed

If you simply whispered in my ear, I know that I would have to hold back before I Blast

With a Voice like yours, you could calm an alpha lion in the Jungle

You could make the most confident man lose his thought process and start to Mumble

Believe me when I say the sound of your Voice is Unsurpassed

So if we ever get to that point where we're smashed together like Ken and Barbie, please don't talk shit because I know I won't Last

IamKnowOne..

They say Beauty is in the Eye of the Beholder

Although I've never seen such Beauty in all of my days

It wasn't her inner beauty, that instantly made me feel like I wanted to Hold Her

She's such an Intellectual Savage

So she loves it when a man simply challenges her Brain, instead of thinking that his money will give him the Right of Passage

Beauty is in the Eye of the Beholder

Although she's so astonishing that a blind man can sense her beauty

It's the FACT that her inner being is Sexy Sagaciously, that's Forcing me to want to Comfort and Hold Her

You Sexy Savage..

IamKnowOne..

I Love catering to my Woman, than looking at her charismatic smile when she's Pleased

How would I expect her to be submissive, if I'm not doing my best to fulfill all of her Needs.

I want to Love her from the Outside In

So she'll understand that I initially had to respect her as my Friend

Than as her Heart opens, she'll know that from the very beginning that my intentions was never to Condescend

But to love her as if I'm her Godsend

IamKnowOne...

The First day we met I'm not sure if it was Love at first Sight

But I damn sure wanted to know what your Love was Like

Now that I know, I feel like I'm in a Parallel Universe

Because your Love is so Amazing, that I honestly forgot that you wasn't the

only woman on Earth

IamKnowOne..

You're so incredibly Breathtaking, as you walk I can see your Melanin being Flooded by Sun Rays

No Woman in the World is Perfect

But the ravishing Scent, that travels behind the path that you walk, is more than Perfect

A Scent that could Bring a Dead Rose back to Life

A rare sumptuous delicate Being that you would undoubtedly Die for, just to have her in your Life

There is No Perfect woman in this World

But she's the Sole Perfection I need in my World

IamKnowOne..

Me without You is like taking the V out of Love

I would unambiguously feel Loe until my Ending Days

Me without You would be like trying to find That single V while searching

through a 100 acre Maze

Impossible, just like Me without You

My mission in Life would be Impossible

IamKnowOne..

I want to Write a Dope ass love Song

So perplexing that she'll cry with joy and hold me all night Long

I want to write a Dope ass love Song

To make her feel so connected, that even when I'm not in her presence she'll want to touch herself all night Long

I want to write a Dope ass love Song

So some of these dudes can humble themselves, pay attention not Fuck but make love to their women all night Long

I want to write a Dope ass love Song

Because some men act like they don't have feelings, they'll never be affectionate, and it doesn't matter how much you love him, he'll keep treating you Wrong

I want to write a Dope ass love Song

Because you deserve to know that I care, instead of me making you feel like you did something Wrong

I want to write a Dope ass love Song

To tell you that I'll never take you for granted and your pain will become my pain, and We can cry together all night Long

I want to write a Dope ass love Song

To tell you if I ever allowed myself to cheat on you, I'll Kill myself because that's not loving you it's Wrong

I want to write a Dope ass love Song

Because if I don't do everything humanly possible to please you, Than you should be Gone.

IamKnowOne..

To have and to Hold

Until we're wrinkled and Old

Smiling about our life, because we no longer have two but a United Soul

When I can look you and your eyes and feel your Pain

Because the same Blood that runs through my Heart, runs through your
Veins

IamKnowOne..

I'm a writer, so I talk my Talk

But I can back it up, walking backwards with my cocky walk in the Dark

With ten nocturnal endangered species coming at my Limb

If you just assumed that you were Loving her right, even in the light your sight is Dim

Learn her love languages, get your head out of your own ass and play Less

But for now I'll Say Less

IamKnowOne..

It's Allergy season and some of us are allergic to Love, Yes Indeed

Every time that special person gets close to your Heart, you can't control your Sneeze

But now they're gone, and you're stuffy, your heart aches, and it's hard for you to Breathe

At that instant you realize that it was fresh Love that you were breathing in, so you ask God Please

Give you another chance as the pain drops you to your Knees

IamKnowOne..

I'm addicted to your Smile

I'm addicted to your Style

If you was a Model for Fashion Nova, You would have the internet Shut Down for Awhile..

I know exactly why I'm Hooked on you, and Wow, please allow me to Bow..

I'll show the world by putting your Gorgeous face on all of my social media Profiles

The mere thought of loving you, just drives me foolishly Wild

IamKnowOne..

Thanks My Queen, I Appreciate you Mind Body and Soul

And the three together controls the way my Heart releases blood Flow

Which now has me Feening for your Love Essence and Presence

If you could take a picture of my Whole Feelings right now, they're so Happy and bright they're Fluorescent

Hey You, I Do I Do I Do Deeply Appreciate You

IamKnowOne..

LOVING YOU

As I wake up in the morning holding all of that Sexiness in my arms

I'm watching you as you Sleep

And you look so Beautiful laying there beside me, but because you're a very strong and intelligent woman, every day I pray the lord your Soul to Keep

But now I know you're ready for Breakfast, Mimosa to start, than bacon with your favorite French toast

Just Relax Enjoy being Spoiled, let me continue showing you why I Love you the Most

To Love you is to know You

And from that look in your Gorgeous eyes

At this very moment I know you just want me to Hold You

But check it, I just bought something Sexy for your feet that's Red at the bottom of the Sole

But buying materialistic things is Priceless when you're In Love with the Woman that has the key to your Soul

See Loving you is Effortless

And I will do everything I can not to Deceive

Because every time you leave out the Front Door it's hard for me to Breathe

IamKnowOne...

I Think I'm Fucking with Her Why?

She's so damn Dope and Amazingly Fly

Her Beauty is so Natural Why?

A Gorgeous Angel, looking like she fell from the Sky

The only Star I let Gratify my Eyes

She's so Damn Sexy and her Aura keeps me High

I vow to Love her, never lie or make her Cry

But If she won't Love me, I might as well Die

NOW I'm Unfuckwittable

Goodbye Goodbye Goodbye..

IamKnowOne..

I can't Stop thinking about our brief moment of Contact

Our eyes connected, than I instantly had to keep my heart palpitations on Track

You had a certain radiance about your skin tone, an alluring glow that was stamping the Earth with phosphorescence

That very moment you passed me By

It almost seemed like a shadow of your Beauty was left Behind, I was so amazed that I kept staring up at the Sky

And it appeared as if the Sun was starting to set but somehow shining only on your Beauty

Or was it your Booty

Nevertheless I can't stop thinking about the day that I'll run into you Again

Trying to persuade myself not to be afraid, I'm very confident but at that moment looking into your eyes was nothing less than Mesmerizing

Please let her pass me by Again

IamKnowOne..

You're So Wondrously Hot

Every time you speak, the Flesh starts Burning from around my Heart

I want to start a conversation but I might be Dead before I Start

I've never Heard of Suicidal Beauty, when a Man could Kill himself from literally opening up his Heart

Now That's Bona Fide Gorgeousness, but I'm willing to take that Chance

So for once in my Life, I could say that I had a Deadly Romance

In for the life of me, I hope all of your Hotness doesn't Kill me, than maybe I can cool down and finish my Conversation

Than I'll know, it's Truly meant for us to have Relations

IamKnowOne..

I'll Patiently study Every inch of Her body as if I'm getting substantially paid to be her Professional Lover
So Whenever I simply Touch her she'll no that I Professionally Love Her
IamKnowOne..

B's

Beautifully bending beneath borrowed blankets, Brittany's bottom Bounces

Boundaries bored bothered Brian's Bone

Brian Blamed basic blood blockage barriers,

Briefly breaking boozing Brittany's Bounces

Brian's badly backed-up beyond being Bamboozled

Brittany's Blown, Brian begged but bent Bone

IamKnowOne..

In a Perfect World when I simply Hold the Woman that I Love
She'll Feel an Irrefutable Bond as her Veins start to Double Dutch with her Heart
Skipping to a Perfect Beat and Unquestionably knowing that this Man is In Love.
IamKnowOne..

I Love the way you keep your guards up like Floyd Mayweather

And I know you're a true Diva, with Brains and Beauty but dumbass men has made your Heart tougher than Leather

But I've leaned how to jab through life expectations, by watching people trying to box with God

Nevertheless I know that it's a Sin to even think about throwing jabs at Angels, who's always on Guard

But if she's Dope I can gradually jab with Love

And I know you Love the Chase, but it's hard to Run if he can leave you Breathless, without boxing Gloves

So in my Nipsey Hustle Voice, I'll keep pushing while staying ten toes Down

As the Marathon Continues... My Dope Angel And one day you'll see that I have no problem kissing your feet and Bowing Down

IamKnowOne..

Love Tastes like I'm Entering the Gates of Heaven

I'll have an Everlasting Flavor of Happiness because I have your Heart Now

So I've Fulfilled my Obsession

The Taste of Love

Happiness fulfilled from Above.

IamKnowOne..

A mother's Love sounds like, listening to Patti LaBelle on the radio while my mom was still Alive

My mom was crying telling me about her broken relationships, while I was just a boy at the age of Five

But at five when your mom cry, you Cry

And you would do anything to help clear up that pain and emptiness and her Eyes

Patti's voice is so Breathtaking, that it'll make fish feel like they can walk on Land

However listening to my mom cry, while telling me her painful stories, was teaching me how to be a better Man

IamKnowOne...

He was abusing a female family member and I couldn't control my anger

He was Shot once in the Head, Than I threw the Gun and Fled

Please stop the Tears from Falling

My mom Died of Breast Cancer years ago

But I still See her face everyday as our kids Grow

Please Stop the Tears from Falling

They had the Whole World in front of them, and was really looking forward to their Marriage

And Three weeks after, she had a Miscarriage

Please Stop the Tears from Falling

I sold Drugs to Family members that are no longer Alive

And I wish I had at least one more day to Apologize

Please Stop the Tears from Falling

Men hurt women Emotionally and Never tried to understand their Pain

Until the tables were turned, than they wanted to put a bullet in her Brain

Please Stop the Tears from Falling

Her parents thought he was the absolute worst, which was a Misfortune

So they Made her have an Abortion

Please Stop the Tears from Falling

He Loved her unconditionally, and Showed the World without Pride

But he caught her Cheating, So he jumped out in front of a Bus and committed Suicide

Please Stop the Tears from Falling

Her husband just died, and she knew he loved her more than the air that they Breathe

Now every night she prays to keep her sanity

Because she recently found out that she was pregnant, and the Stress keeps making her Bleed

Please Stop the Tears from Falling

As you Walk through the Valley of the shadow of Death, you have to know that God is Calling

And He will Stop the Tears from Falling

IamKnowOne...

First I'm going to Make Love to your Mind

By Caressing your Heart so tight, that you'll almost feel like you're out of Breath

Until you truly understand that I want to Love you as if you're the last woman Left

Than I'll proceed with the little things like massaging your inner Thoughts

By Showing you how much I care about your Wants, Needs and Desires right from the very Start

As you allow my Verbal foreplay to get into your cerebrum, and start giving you a Full body Workout

You'll begin to connect with me Mentally, Emotionally, Than Physically without Doubt

Allowing your Heart to sense that I'm coming from a safe Place

While your Mind is unquestionably enjoying my Love Making, because every time I see you there is always a smile on your Face

Meanwhile You're starting to feel condensation on your inner thighs, as you say to yourself Damn am I that l Dope in a low Voice

While your Mind is getting an unforgettable Loving Feeling from this man that's leaving you no Choice

IamKnowOne..

Every night when I Close my eyes I see your Face

As I'm Smiling racing towards you, I keep falling off of the same cliff at the exact same Place

I appear to be so In Love with this Face that I keep Chasing

Nevertheless I know it's a sign because I continuously Fall, while Never Embracing

IamKnowOne..

A Smorgasbord full of Women at your Leisure

Or a lifetime of Happiness Simply Pleasing Her

Everything at the Buffet looks Sensational

That Beef Tenderloin over there looks very Moist

And Damn That Filet Mignon so Tempting, and Five Stars the Superior Choice

But I'm elated with the Rib Eye

Very ravishing, and I can tell that no man had to Pound on it to make it tender

It's unexploited and never Dry

It Simply Seems Submissively Satisfying so I'll always be ready to taste it, never appearing Shy

I can tell it's exceedingly flavorful, and it doesn't want just any man to stick his knife In

It likes to be seasoned well, and Gracefully Pounded on from beginning to End

Succulent enough for the Juices to have continuous flow, leaving the essence of a Pear

And I know it was tested, so I would love eating it Medium Rare

That Rib Eye is so Obedient that every time it allows me to put my White layers on it

I almost start to Cry

Yes Indeed, there is quite a few enticing selections at this buffet

But as I said I'm elated with the Rib Eye

IamKnowOne..

Love is like the Orgasm that you thought you'd never Have, but consistently try to Seek

You've been pleased in different ways but it never reached its Peak

You knew of people that could satisfy you Well

But you also know that one person that will have you walking through the fires in Hell

Love is a delicate emotional feeling that will have you continuously beating your Head up against inner Walls

Than as the walls get tighter around your head, you start to smile knowing you're in Euphoria

Now your Whole Feelings are Involved

Love is not satisfactory or Perfection

But once you know the feeling is coming, it becomes your life's Obsession

IamKnowOne..

Whenever I think of you, my Heart starts to feel like I ran for Miles

Your Beauty Wow..

I'm to apprehensive to talk, because I know that I would trip over my Words

Your Beauty Wow..

Every time I look into your Eyes, I can see My Smile

And It's very satisfying, simply knowing that picturesque moment will be locked in my head for a While

Your Beauty Wow..

One day I'll tell you, that I know exactly how many eyelashes you have over your right Eye

See I pay attention to all of you, not just that bump above your Thighs

Your Beauty Wow..

IamKnowOne..

The Sky is Falling

Should I commit as many Sins as I Can

Or do I beg for Forgiveness, Knowing it's the End

The Sky is Falling

Do I Party, Lust, and Drink my Day Away

Or Do I get down on my knees in Pray

The Sky is Falling

I can Feel the Devil more and more trying to encourage me to go his Way

But out of nowhere, God jumped out and said Not Today

IamKnowOne..

She's Truly my One Love

Everyday she treats me like a King, so I never felt like I Won Love

I know it was given to me Wholeheartedly, so I'm sure it's not Dumb Love

The sex is always amazing, so I'm absolutely sure that it's not Cum Love

Never will I ever let temptations come in between My Love

It's not a Game, you can't Win Love

But I've Won, because I know she's truly my One Love

IamKnowOne..

Love is not Given

Love is Earned

Love takes patience, consistency and understanding, so I understand that you're Concerned

But When I finish doing everything humanly possible to earn your Love, your soul is going to feel like it's been hit by a Bachelors party Bus

Than as you slowly open your eyes and only see one man, you'll say to yourself, I know that this Love is for Us

IamKnowOne..

The most Powerful Essence on this Universe is a Woman

Powerful enough to have Humans come out of her Body

But for the Life of me I can't understand why they can't have Equality

So it's Permissible when a man wants his needs Fulfilled and put his Penis in a Woman's Vagina

But is very Hard for some Men to work in a major Corporation and Grow Behind Her

But if She's Naked it makes it Easy for a Man to want to Grow Behind Her

But She's Unreservedly Amazing and Every way so Why should Her Sex Define Her

Female Emancipation

KEEP PUSHING..

IamKnowOne...

She said that her man had Alien levels of Toxicity

She said that she loved him to no End

But consistently being treated like his Bitch was accelerating the lost of her Dignity

She started deeply testing her integrity, but seeing herself with another man, was like trying to see through heavy fog on the Red Sea

I knew with my Whole heart that she deserved so much More

But why did she allow herself to continuously be treated like a bottom Whore

I'm sure there's a man out there that will hold her, care for her, cherish her and most certainly Adore

You shouldn't be with a man and still feel lonely, get your eyes off of that sick bastard, and your heart off of the Floor

In Real Life there's a Real man coming for you, that will unquestionably even the Score

IamKnowOne...

I am a Preadator for love, a natural Savage for the woman that I'm sure could give me Truelove

Never overbearing, just consistent and my persistence for our Coexistence

Giving her enough distance, to allow her whole feelings to grow without Resistance

But my Predation, is solely for our relations, but take your time and take in all of your Observations

Because once you start falling your whole heart will shatter with any thought of Separation

Nevertheless my dedication and determination

will continuously Eat a predatory hole in your soul without Hesitation

Than you'll realize this is where your Love should have always shown its Concentration

I am Gods Creation, I will never fear women's temptation, and I'll always be hungry for only your Adoration

IamKnowOne..

I wish that I could take the Pain Away

I wish that we could dance together Naked in the rain, until God washes the Pain Away

I wish that I could take the Pain Away

I wish that I could hold you so tight throughout the night, until you realize nothing else in this entire World could Ever feel so Right

I wish that I could take the Pain Away

One day my Love will simply be enough, but for now I'll continue to get down on my knees and pray for Us

I wish that I could take the Pain Away

One day you'll wake up in my arms and realize, that there is no more pain Today

And that I'm the One, that's going to love you unconditional, the Real life Way.

IamKnowOne..

Sometimes you Feel like Life is just to Preposterous

But God will Never Put you in a Maze that you can't get out of

You Know the Path you need to take, but you Keep turning Left

When you know you Need to turn Right

You're Ignoring your Faith and Deranging your Life

When All along you know Right

IamKnowOne..

Bonjour comment allez-vous

I'm Fine, now that I've been Embraced by your Beauty

Je suis désolé est-ce que vous parlez français

A little, but I do Speak Love and from the look in your eyes so do You

IamKnowOne..

To Love Her is to Know Her

Her Favorite Color, Favorite Food, Favorite Show on TV

Do She like to Cuddle? Walk holding Hands

Do you Touch her Mentally

If you Truly Love Her, than you Know Her Heart

Consistency along with the Little things that are Sincerely Meant

So Don't Promise Her the House with the White Picket Fence

When you Know you just want to Rent

IamKnowOne..

I want to Love You

I want to Hold You

I want to Protect You

I want to Show You off to the World

OH what an Amazing Feeling it would be Knowing that you're My Girl

We wouldn't have time to Argue

I would be to busy trying to create Special moments of simply Enjoying You

I want to watch Comedies creating Our own memories of Laughter

I want to Learn All of your Likes and Dislikes so I can Surprise You with

Gifts of Love without creating a Disaster

I Don't Know or Care How You was Loved in the Past

I just know I'm going to do Everything in My Power to Treat you like the

Queen that You are

Until your Heart Knows I'm the Last

Hey You, I Unambiguously Want To

IamKnowOne..

A Woman's Worth

We have to Motivate our Women and Stop tearing them Down

You have to understand the True meaning of a Woman's worth to keep her coming Around

Never say there's No man out there that's going to treat you like Me

Because if you Truly gave her your Unconditional Love, that would be something without saying that she could See

Let your Actions speak, by the wonderful things you say and do for this woman

Be her Godsend

We have to stop saying Uninspiring words that will wound her until the End

I would like to Apologize to All the women who didn't get what they were Worth

Men are a little bit slower than you and without you here, we couldn't make it on this Earth

You have the Blessing of bringing what will become a man on this Earth

So you should Undeniably get more than you're Worth

IamKnowOne..

The Confidence of a Goddess, she has No Insecurities

But I was so impressed by her Intellectual Beauty

That her Physical Appearance didn't matter

She wasn't trying to be ♡ Liked by Every man in the World

She only needed one man to Stick his DM in her Inbox

Real Love Matters

IamKnowOne..

How do you chase an Angel

She has huge wings and blessings from Heaven all year Round

Every time I hear her desirable voice I want to sprint towards the Sound

How do you chase an Angel

Whenever I see her face, I simply want to call her Your Grace and Bow Down

How do you chase an Angel

She's so Classy and Gorgeous with enough elegance to be Queen of her own Land

But my apologies I'm selfish, so I would Love for her to be Queen for just this Man

How do you chase an Angel

It's preposterous, she has to accept you in her Heart

So keep your feelings consistent, and Pray to God for a head Start

IamKnowOne..

She's the epitome of my Dream Girl, and she got me Falling

I'm Falling and I can't Help It

When I asked God for a sign, my phone started ringing, guess who's Calling

I'm Falling and I can't Help It

Just the notion of her Smile, takes me from

Stressed to Calming

I'm Falling and I can't Help It

I wouldn't care if I had to spend the rest of my days in, with this woman

that's So Amazing

I'm Falling and I can't Help It

She owns my whole soul, and she doesn't even know how deep my heart is In

I'm Falling and I can't Help It

Bae, You're a little Hood, but It Hit Different when your Brain matches the

savage in your Beauty

I can't Help it I'm Falling..

My whole feelings craves your love as my heart awaits anxiously Crawling

IamKnowOne..

My Desires are not to Hurt you, My Desires are to consistently Love and Respect you, until your Whole Heart has feelings that it never felt Before

This is in no way what so ever a game to me, I'm not looking for another notch on my belt to achieve the highest Score

I'm simply trying to be with the woman that I Adore

Can you hear me Bae? My Work ethics when it comes to Love is unequivocal for Sure

You have the key, just patiently waiting for you to open the Door

IamKnowOne..

Wherever you want me to go, I'll Go

I haven't been to Church in years, but with you I'll sit in the front Row

So you can see that I'm willing to put God first, than watch our Love Grow

My anxiety goes crazy on the days that I'm blessed enough to see your Face

I'm just so Amazed that your whole heart is giving in, because it loves the way I Chase

There's only one of You on this Entire Earth

And I'm willing to consistently show you what your Love is Worth

IamKnowOne..

Humbled Through Pain

See as a young man you're Predictable

And you Think with your Predictable

Most young men don't know how to care for, Love or understand a Woman's needs and Desires

The only thing on their minds. is what they can Acquire

Most young women are thinking about how they can secure their Future without a whole lot of Friction

But most young Men are thinking about how many women they can Infiltrate with their Prediction

Unanticipatedly through life lessons you learn how to listen be abating, and when it comes to something important to her never keep her Waiting

As most Men mature they show more perseverance with their continuity in Loving and Respecting their Women as a Whole

We learn not to take you for Granted, to Stop thinking with our Predictions and how to brush your Soul

As we mature, we are not the same boys we were running around focusing only on our Predictions

We understand that you need to be held, Loved, lots of quality time and Attention

Now when you talk we don't just hear it we Listen

And only after these things are Done is when we get to exercise our Prediction

As young men most of us are immature disrespectful and we can seem Insane

Until we find the right one, that makes our heart hurt when we're wrong and helps us understand True emotional Pain

IamKnowOne..

That Body makes me feel so demented that I just want to Gently reconstruct her inner Walls

Just the thought of her coming near me, is making me want to Grab her, Choke her, and drive up against her Walls

And who told her to keep wearing that Damn Chanel No Five

It makes me want to take her in the parking garage and eat her Ass Alive

If I ever get the chance, I'll slowly put it In

than creatively drive around her Walls as if I have road Rage

Than make her feel so good that she'd wish she read the Whole book on me, not just one damn Page

Start telling her how her aura makes me feel so incredibly Untamed

Start talking very provocatively, as the feeling vividly makes me scream her Name

Start pulling her hair while Whispering in her ear, that now is Not the time to make Love

As we start walking towards the wall and I give her a benevolent Shove

Than I Grab her, pull her close, get excited and Leave skid marks on her walls

While her back is up against the wall

Than tell her how her sex appeal is calling the Beast out of Me

As I give her eye contact and she sluggishly taps out, smiles and makes a considerable Plea

IamKnowOne...

#Dope Angel

Did you ever feel like you wanted to jump to your Death

Than you had an encounter with a Dope Angel that made you feel so amazing,

that you Really almost lost your Breath

Simply Her presence alone makes you feel so High that you're Flying with

Angels

A feeling as such could never be Painful

You don't need alcohol or Drugs

Simply her Aura makes you feel Loved

It Will unquestionably be the best High of your life, never Baneful

She's so miraculously Dope, with the Grace and Face of an Angel

#dope angel

IamKnowOne..

Wow, you're Gorgeous and you smell so Deliciously Amazing

I'm sure every time you cross a mans path, it'll be nothing less than Captivating

What's that you have on, is that the New instant Pregnancy by Chanel no 5..No Lol..

Em Em Em, such a Beautiful woman with an alluring Smell

I know today is Wednesday, but Damn you smell like everyday is Hump Day IamKnowOne..

DEFENSE ON 3

Life is Tough, but I keep my Guards up as if I'm playing Ball

I know Defense is my Best Offense

And them dudes have a Draco, and they keep chanting it's their World after All

But my team stay in shape it's Protocol

Besides we stay on fire, like an open wound doused with rubbing Alcohol

I start my day off with the Team running Suicides

We try to stay Motivated and keep the Blood flowing, so no one contemplates Suicide

Than I decide the Defense for the Day

I know how much Artillery we have, so we're more than OK

I don't know if I'm going with the 1 2 2, the 2 3 press or the Diamond and 1

Because out of the whole team, we know the Shooter is the only One

So we'll still fake them out with a Full court Press

Although we know their shooter is their Best

So I'll put my Center at the top of the Key

And he can observe where everyone will Be

Than when the shooter thinks he can break the Press

My 2 guard will set a pick, while my point guard steals the ball

Now the whole team looks Distressed, but I smell Success

The Draco Isn't good if you don't know how to use it, Think and use your Team

This wasn't even a hostile takeover, Easy Dunk Game Over

IamKnowOne..

I just want to know your ETA

There is no other man in the world like me, why don't you come over and let me show you Today

I just want to know your ETA

I don't know how much he loved you, but I Promise you, you'll be treated so Amazingly good, that you'll forget his name by the end of the Day

I just want to know your ETA

After I cook dinner for you, while waiting on you hand and Foot

We can discuss our Love languages, as you start to think Damn, does he have the magic Book

I just want to know your ETA

Because after a day of being treated like the last Angel on earth, you'll be begging me to Stay

So whenever you're ready Gorgeous,

I just want to know your ETA

IamKnowOne..

She said I made Love amazing and Fun

And after the First time we made Love, she knew that I was the One

She said that Loving me was the most Effortless thing she's ever done in her entire Life

But I thought that was very facetious, because I already knew that she was a lying cheating manipulative Wife

Than she said that cheating on me would hurt her so bad that she would have to take her own Life

So as I walked into the kitchen to get the Biggest and Sharpest Knife

I also came back with the information about her Double Life

I showed her the information from the hotel and restaurant where she Ate

She immediately cried, tried to say that she was sorry, but no one cheats by Mistake

And Since it was so easy for you to let someone stick it in

I'm going to give you the fucking knife and watch you Begin

Oh by the way, it'll be easier if you start on the left side of your Chest

It's that organ that helps you Love, it's Effortless

IamKnowOne..

I can tell by your Hustle, that you're very Formidable

One day doesn't determine your outcome

Keep Pushing, Smile Hold your head up

We don't do Pitiful

I can tell that you Aspire becoming the Best

God put challenges in our path for a reason

Just keep being righteous

Some of life lessons are merely a Test

Keep Pushing, Smile Hold your head up

Through God We don't do Stress

KEEP PUSHING.

IamKnowOne..

The Sun is starting to set, as the Moon rises with its Crown

As the night is almost upon us, Evil lurks throughout the Town

When the Nocturnal creatures feels it's easiest to Walk

Because even with Keen eyes we can't see shadows in the Dark

Be aware as you go about your Night

Your grass is beautifully trimmed, but sometimes it's hard to see a snake unless it Bites

Although you're moving freely throughout the Town

Walk with Humbled legs because the Moon wears the Immoral Crown

Watch how you treat people because what goes around might come out of the shadows and put you Down

IamKnowOne..

I think I'm getting close to carving my claws through her Heart-Freddy

She was starting to open up to me in a Nightmarish Way, but now she's Ready

Than said if I you hurt me Bastard it will get Deadly

So from 7pm to 7am I better not even think about doing anything Absurd

Because she had feelings for me that she never felt before and she wasn't afraid to Purge

And if I had even a pint sized thought of fucking up our Relations

Than she guaranteed me that this will be my Final Destination

She said please take care of my Heart, and recognize the reality that you're Facing

Because she wasn't afraid to put a machete through my Heart-Jason IamKnowOne..

She said she Wish there was an Angel to take the Pain Away

His Love was so Amazing, that in the Winter even the Birds wanted to Stay

She use to suffer from Winter Depression because of the Sunset Time

However when He's in her presence, He's her walking ray of Sunshine

So The season didn't matter, her Heart Felt Summer all the Time

He Treated Her very Exceptional, she knew that his love would assuredly last a Lifetime

She's so In Love with this Man that it's causing her Pain

She Feels if He ever leaves her, she'll undeniably go Insane

Than she realizes she just have to get over her fears, since that eternal Sunshine was All that she Dreamed Of

And undoubtedly sent to her from her Angels Above

Sometimes it might Rain, But it's Not Worth Losing your One True Love.

IamKnowOne..

Trying to create Moisture from Poetic Expressions

I know you can't hear me, but through my words I'm Caressing

Your Sexual Fantasies and inner most thoughts of being with Me

Even if your hands were tied, you could still feel this overwhelming passion

coming from Me

Physically I'm not there but Mentality I'm all in

Close your eyes and lets Begin

I start by gently rubbing the bottom of your Foot

Than I Glance in your Eyes and see a fulfilled Look

I have a slight Foot fetish so I start kissing your Toes

your face look surprised

I got this just keep your Eyes Closed

I'm gently kissing on your lower leg moving up towards your inner Thigh

I think I see your Box Pulsating can you tell me Why?

Ok I know you're Box is calling, and Believe you Me

By the time you reach your Pinnacle every inch of your body will belong to

Me

Let's take our time Relax

Matter of fact turn over let my fingers get acquainted with your Back

Let me massage your stress Away

But damn looking at your Gorgeous Body is making my Soldier want to come out and Play

But with age comes Patients and when I finish learning your Body

I'm going to patiently Tear that ass up

And make your Body my Body

I'm sorry I sound Cocky

But I've always been Confident in my Capabilities so Please (SMHIMH) don't try Me....

IamKnowOne...

She stands out like the Stars and the Clouds

Her hustle is impeccable, she makes me incredibly Proud

She does her best to over achieve, even on the smallest task she's working On

That's why I make it my business to compliment and support her, because I know I'm her Proton

The most beautiful Stars shines at Night

Except my Star that unexpectedly shines throughout the Daylight

Keep shining babe, like the Sun when it's one hundred Degrees

I'll always be supportive like the dirt to the Trees

Its my obligation to help you Grow

Because with you, touching the Clouds seems abundantly Possible

IamKnowOne..

Hello Beautiful, can you Respect me for my Wicked ways

I'm a Wild Boy, but Love Calms me Like a Cool Breeze during Summer Days

Your eyes are Remarkably mesmerizing

I think you have a Spell on Me

Because Holding You in my Arms is All I See

My mentality use to be stuck on my Bad Boy Ways

But to be Loved by such a Woman would indisputably deserve Praise

IamKnowOne..

Every time I see her Face, I instantly Smile

My stomach Drops, and I get a little nervous for a While

She has the Poise of a Princess, the style of a Fashion Designer, the Face of a Goddess, the Walk of a Model, simply a Bombshell

With enough sex appeal to make you want to ejaculate on Yourself, than Confidently Scream Her name and Emphatically Yell

Her personality is so infectious, that if you're around her you'll just want to stare and pay Attention

I'm Sorry, but did I Mention

I'm nervous Again, the essence of that Woman

She's a Masterpiece, a Beautiful work of Art, A Strong Insightful Ravishing Woman

IamKnowOne..

My Buddy works Nights, He got off early one night and his Wife said she wanted to Role Play

She said I'll be a Teacher and you can be a Fireman

He was Excited, his Wife was getting Kinky so he said Cool sounds like a Plan

So they got Dressed for the Occasion

Had a few glasses of Wine than his Wife started after a little Persuasion

She said Bring that Ass here and put out Mrs. Jones Fire. Before I give you extra Homework

He said I'm Here Beautiful and I'm about to show you how this Long Hose Work

Minutes later, She sighs and said I Wasted 3 minutes of my life on mediocre Ding a Ling

WELL OK I'm going to get something to drink

Do you need Anything

Yes for you to get that bottle of Stamina behind the O.J

Yeah she got Jokes but I feel Good I'm OK

Hey Son why are you still Awake

Hey Dad I'm sorry I know it's Late

But around this time Every Night

Mom is usually in the room Screaming for Hours

Saying Damn this Big Hose is ALRIGHT

Than I see the neighbor leave with his Fireman's uniform looking like he just lost a Fight

Damn Really, LoFuckingL

IamKnowOne..

That Day in August

That Mind bending day in August as an Angel was being Sworn In

The Sun was at its brightest, as the birds were chirping and playing throughout the Morning

I heard the Sky never looked so enticing, as there were rumors of Angels Dancing

They said it seemed like every Butterfly in the World, was outside the window Glancing

New wings were being formed, and that's Entrancing

Than came the crying and screaming from a Gorgeous baby Girl

That Was the Alluring sound of an Angel entering this troublesome yet meaningful World

Her Fate was inevitable, but even through death she was destined to Win

My Mom, my Homie, my Best Friend

Deborah McGowan. In God We Trust

As He knew there was an Angel being born That day in August

8/22/1958-2/22/2000

IamKnowOne.. IamDebbie'sSon

Printed in the United States
By Bookmasters